*And behold,
I am with you always,
even to the end of the world.*

Matthew 28:20

I Am With You Always

A *Living Faith* Prayer Companion

Psalm Versions by
Elizabeth-Anne Vanek

Edited by
Mark Neilsen

Illustrations by
Annie Scheumbauer

Introduction by
*Rev. John Catoir,
Director of* The Christophers

CREATIVE COMMUNICATIONS FOR THE PARISH, INC.
ST. LOUIS, MISSOURI

Imprimatur:
Monsignor Maurice F. Byrne
Vice Chancellor, Archdiocese of St. Louis

Copyright © 1991 by
Creative Communications for the Parish

All Rights Reserved. No part of this book may be reproduced or republished in any manner without written permission. Send all inquiries to:

Creative Communications for the Parish
10300 Watson Road
St. Louis, MO 63127-1187

ISBN number: 0-9629585-0-6

Cover by Annie Scheumbauer

Printed in the United States of America

Contents

Foreword — vii

Introduction — ix

Morning, Noon & Night
　Daily Prayers — 1

Bless the Lord, O My Soul
　Prayers of Praise, Joy & Thanksgiving — 25

My Hope Is In You, My God
　Prayers of Hope & Trust in Times of Doubt — 43

Fear Not, I Am With You
　Prayers in Time of Illness — 61

For The Sake Of Others
　Prayers of Intercession — 77

Forgive Me, I Have Sinned
　Prayers of Penitence — 93

Dwelling As One
　Prayers for the Family — 105

I Am The Life
　Prayers of Mourning — 121

Christ Our Light
　Prayers for the Church Year — 133

My God & My All
　Special Devotions — 153

Acknowledgments — 177

Index of Authors — 179

Foreword

Readers of *Living Faith*, the booklet of daily Catholic devotions, have from time to time thanked us for the prayers in the back of each issue and asked for more. This volume is intended to meet that request, to be a companion volume throughout the year and throughout the seasons of one's life.

Designed for use by all members of the praying Church, this book contains a variety of prayers, from the very personal to the general, the traditional to the contemporary. What they have in common is their recognition of God as the source of all that is good.

St. Paul tells us that the Spirit prays in us, offering groans and sighs when words are not available. Truly, God is the source of all genuine prayer. Is God also the source of all genuine prayer *books*? We hope so.

May God continue to nurture the life of Christ in you and may your prayers be confident, fervent and enduring.

Mark Neilsen

Introduction

VOCAL PRAYER is a lifting of the mind and heart to God through written words. Whether you are alone, or attending a liturgy, whether you are asking for something or thanking God, pleading for forgiveness, or making reparation for sins, the goal of vocal prayer is to give yourself to God.

Mental prayer is either wordless contemplation or a spontaneous prayer from the heart. When Jesus responded to the question "Teach us how to pray," he taught his disciples a vocal prayer, the "Our Father." This timeless prayer establishes for us the proper disposition, which is openness to God: "Thy Kingdom come...." Once the formalities are completed the pleading begins: "Give... Forgive...Do not let us be tempted beyond our strength...Deliver us from evil." These are serious requests that presuppose our faith in God's love. In fact, they require full trust and confidence.

We believe that God really hears our

Introduction

prayers and answers them. God has answered so many of my prayers I can't keep track of them. One of my favorite memories of God's intervention was with a cousin of mine named Vincent Wagner. Vincent developed a severe case of rheumatoid arthritis in his early 20's. His life was a sea of pain and my heart went out to him. He had become quite bitter with no hope of ever marrying. "Who would have me?" he would say. "Look at me, I'm a wreck. I can't work on a regular basis. I can't walk half of the time. With this miserable body of mine, I would be a burden to any woman. It wouldn't be fair."

He was angry with God and with himself, and who could blame him? I felt so sorry for him. All I could do was pray for him, hoping that he'd meet someone who would love him well. When I told him that I was praying for that intention, he just scoffed.

Years later he did marry a wonderful woman named Marge, and his attitude toward life changed completely. In spite of recurring pain, he became a cheerful person and found real happiness.

Introduction

Time passed and one night at a family reunion, he leaned over to me and whispered, "Marge and I have you to thank for bringing us together." I was stunned: "Me? What do you mean?" I thought he was referring to my prayers. "Don't you remember?" he said. "You introduced us." My jaw dropped. I had absolutely no recollection of it. He told me it was at a family wedding, she was a bridesmaid, and apparently I had introduced them in passing. I had no intention of matching them up since Marge was about 16 years younger than he.

Now as I look back on this whole story, I see God's sense of humor. I prayed that Vincent would meet someone, and God not only answered my prayer, but arranged it so that I would introduce Vincent to his future bride. I marvel at God's wonderful imagination.

It's important to have confidence in the Lord when you pray. He listens to your prayers with deepest love. You have in your hand a little prayer book, prepared by the editors of *Living Faith* magazine. It contains some simple, straightforward prayers of praise, petition and penance. The words

Introduction

are not fancy, but their meaning is profound.

Listen to the words of Jesus as he instructs you in the art of praying:

> "I tell you the truth, the Father will give you anything you ask in my name. Ask, and receive, that your joy may be full."
> *John 16:23-24*

> "Ask, and you shall receive; seek, and you shall find; knock and it shall be open to you."
> *Matthew 7:7*

> "What you want will be done for you."
> *Matthew 15:28*

> "Your Father knows you need many things. Put His kingdom first in your life and He will provide for you."
> *Luke 12:30-31*

> "Will God not judge in favor of his own people who cry to him for help day and night? Will he be slow to help them? I tell you, he will judge in their favor and do it quickly."
> *Luke 18:7-8*

The words of Jesus are important to us; so, too, are the words we speak to him. Vocal prayer gives us words that help in guiding and directing our thoughts. Clarity

Introduction

of expression is of value in any relationship. And yet, true prayer is not merely "thinking" orderly thoughts. True prayer is in the will to give yourself to God!

The best disposition of the soul is one of openness to the Holy Spirit. We express our vulnerability and our deepest spiritual yearnings. Even if our thoughts wander or our emotions flounder during prayer, we need not be troubled, because true prayer is in the will. There is no need to try to force feelings of any kind. By reading your favorite prayers, you guide your thoughts gently and trust in the Lord.

Sometimes when I pray my breviary, I sense that I am scanning the Psalms too quickly. It would take hours to pray the daily Divine Office in a truly meditative way. There are too many profound thoughts to consider in one reading. Nevertheless, I reassure myself continually that I am really praying, not because my mind is focused on every word, but because of my continuous intention to give myself to God. I do not try to force any feelings of love or devotion. They may come automatically; if so, that's to the good, but feelings are not

Introduction

essential to prayer. At times I have warm feelings, but often my feelings are dry. There have been a few times in my life when I was overpowered by a vibrant experience of God's presence, but such exaltation is rare. Good feelings are not the essence of good prayer; self-giving and an awareness of God's presence is.

When I read prayers, sometimes my eyes may scan life after line, sometimes I pick up the meaning, sometimes I drift off into a desire of the heart. The words are not chains that bind me; they are springboards that send my spirit soaring. I let go of the words whenever that happens. My desire to surrender to God is always there even when I am not aware of it. And because this desire is constant, I know that I pray without ceasing. My will remains fixed on God even in moments when I don't advert to God at all. At least that's what I try to do.

What about God's silence? If I had to rely on feedback from God in order to be sure I was praying well, I'd be miserable. You have to understand that God is a silent lover. His silence does not, however, mean he is absent. Whether you feel him or not,

Introduction

God is unchanging love.

When you rely on the fact that true prayer is in the will, you gain an edge in handling your emotions. There is no universal "right way to pray." Abbot John Chapman, a noted English spiritual writer who died in 1931 used to say: "The only way to pray well is to pray often."

Try to forget yourself. God's love is flowing in and around us all the time. The only thing that you have to do is relax and accept it.

I wish you well with your prayers.

May Jesus be your strength and your joy.

Rev. John Catoir
February 15, 1991

Morning, Noon & Night
Daily Prayers

Morning, Noon and Night

Psalm 1

HAPPY ARE they
who ignore misleading advice,
avoiding the path of sin
and the company of scoffers;
they delight in your law, O God,
meditating on it night and day.

They are like trees
planted near running water,
laden with summer fruits,
green-leafed into the fall.
All they do yields a harvest;
not so for the wicked.

No, the wicked are like wind-scattered
husks; they will not stand firm
at judgment.
God, you shelter the just,
but the wicked will waste away. †

Morning, Noon and Night

GOOD MORNING, dear God! Refreshed from the good night's sleep you gave me, I am ready now to try to see your love in my life and to share it. Help me to see each part of this day in a new way, just as all seems fresh, new, alive to me this morning.
Lord, if it be your will, let the enthusiasm and joy of this morning carry me through the day to share your love with all those I meet. †

Jean Royer

Morning, Noon and Night

A Morning Offering

O JESUS, THROUGH the Immaculate Heart of Mary,
I offer you my prayers, works, joys and
sufferings of this day,
in union with the Holy Sacrifice of the
Mass throughout the world.
I offer them
for all the intentions of your
Sacred Heart:
the salvation of souls,
in reparation for sin,
and the reunion of all Christians.
I offer them for all the intentions of the
Holy Father, our bishops, the
Apostleship of prayer and in particular
for [*name your intentions*]. ✝

Morning, Noon and Night

EVERYTHING I have, my God,
comes from you.
Everything I am is yours as well.
I thank you for these gifts—the gift of
myself and of my family and friends,
the gift of my home and
all that is within it,
the gift of my talents and
all that I do.
Accept these gifts, O God,
as my offering to you. I spread them on
the altar of this day and ask that you
will smile on them. †
Elizabeth-Anne Vanek

Morning, Noon and Night

THE SUN HAS risen, God.
Night's shadows have fled.
The birds announce a new day.
Here I am, ready to do your will.
Here I am, ready to find you
in every moment, to see you in every
person that I meet.
I offer you this day
which you have given me.
I praise you for this morning and for all
the mornings of my life.
Be with me in every trial and
in every joy; do not let me
lose sight of you.
Watch over me; keep me safe.
I praise you, God; I thank you. †
Elizabeth-Anne Vanek

Morning, Noon and Night

WE GIVE YOU heartfelt thanks, heavenly Father, for the rest of the past night, and for the gift of a new day with its opportunities of living to your glory. May we so pass its hours in the perfect freedom of your service that, when evening comes, we may again give you thanks, through Jesus Christ our Lord. †
Office of the Orthodox Church

Morning, Noon and Night

Midday Prayers

O GOD, GRANT me a moment to reflect on your gift to me of this day. Help me to see your touch in all that has already happened and to hope that you will be with me in all that is still coming my way. For the tasks you have given me and for strength to face them,
I thank you, Lord.
For these moments of peace and
for all the ways you keep me going
whether I am aware of them or not,
I give you thanks. †

Mark Neilsen

The Angelus

THE ANGEL of the Lord declared unto Mary:
And she conceived of the Holy Spirit.
Hail Mary...

Morning, Noon and Night

Behold the handmaid of the Lord:
Be it done to me according to your word.
Hail Mary...

And the Word was made flesh:
And dwelt among us.
Hail Mary...

Pray for us, O Holy mother of God:
That we may be made worthy of the
promises of Christ.

Let us pray:
Pour forth, we beseech you, O Lord,
your grace into our hearts, that we
to whom the incarnation of Christ,
your Son, was made known by
the message of an angel,
may be brought by his passion
and cross to the glory of his resurrection,
through the same Christ our Lord. †

Morning, Noon and Night

JESUS, BE NEAR ME in this bustle
of activity and noise today.
When I become absorbed in myself,
turn my attention to you and to the
needs of those around me
so that I can give away some of the
goodness you have given me.
Show me the right path for
the remainder of this day and
refresh me so I can go on renewed
to try to do your will.
Help me to remember that you are
the Source of all life,
the Judge of all success,
and the Measure of all that is good. †
Mark Neilsen

Morning, Noon and Night

An Evening Remembrance

I WANT TO end this day
in your company.
There is much my heart wants
to tell you.
You have been with me all
through this day;
shall we go over our time together?

Thank you
for this day of life,
for all that it brought me—
the opportunities I was given,
the people I met,
the conversations I had,
the knowledge I gained,
the love I gave and received.

I look back upon the joys I experienced,
at the tasks I was able to complete,
at the satisfaction this day brought me.

Morning, Noon and Night

I also look at my disappointments
and failures,
at the jobs left unfinished,
at the pain I caused,
at the good I left undone,
at the memories that still hurt.
Open my eyes to the wonders you
worked today in the world and in me.
Open my heart to accept
your pardon and your peace.
Teach me to end this day
in trustful surrender.

In you I trust.
To you I belong.
To your love I entrust
all those who died today
and their dear ones who mourn;
and those who are on their deathbed
right now.

No one is lost to your sight;
may they also be present to my heart:
those who work all night; all travelers

Morning, Noon and Night

and those in charge of their safety;
all those who had a difficult day,
or fear the oncoming night;
those in pain, and those
who are too lonely to rest or to pray.

May these evening hours prepare me
for the great evening of my life,
when I will look back on life's day,
and find no words
to thank you
for all the love I will have received. †

Joe Mannath, S.D.B.

Canticle of Simeon

NOW, MASTER, you may let your servant go in peace, according to your word, for my eyes have seen your salvation, which you prepared in the sight of all the peoples, a light for revelation to the Gentiles, and the glory of your people Israel. †

Luke 2:29-32

Morning, Noon and Night

O GOD of the daylight and
of the darkness,
be our light tonight.
May we know your loving presence
as we seek rest and refreshment from
the toils of the day.
Comfort us in your embrace.
We thank you for all the joys
you have given us this day and
for guiding us through the rough spots.
Forgive us the times we failed
to live lovingly.
Guard our sleep that we may awake
tomorrow ready to love and serve you. †
Jean Royer

Morning, Noon and Night

HOLY SPIRIT, I thank you for being with me this day, for all the happiness your will has brought, and for all the toil and hardship I have had to accept. Forgive me for the times when I have forgotten you amid the cares of the day. Forgive me also if I have not accepted any suffering in the same spirit as Christ my Lord.
Help me to rest in peace tonight, that I may wake truly refreshed and willing to spend a new day in your service.
Grant that when I close my eyes for the last time in this world, I may wake in the joy of your presence. †

Living Faith

PROTECT us, Lord, as we stay awake; watch over us as we sleep, that awake we may keep watch with Christ, and asleep, rest in his peace. †

Liturgy of the Hours

Morning, Noon and Night

WATCH, O LORD, those who wake or watch or weep tonight, and give your angels and saints charge over those who sleep.
Tend your sick ones, O Lord Christ. Rest your weary ones, bless your dying ones, soothe your suffering ones, pity your afflicted ones, shield your joyous ones, and all for your love's sake. †

St. Augustine

Before Meals

BLESS US, O Lord, and these your gifts which we are about to receive from your bounty, through Christ our Lord. †

Morning, Noon and Night

After Meals

WE GIVE you thanks, Almighty God, for all your benefits which we have received from your bounty, through Christ our Lord. ✝

The Lord's Prayer (traditional)

OUR FATHER, who art in heaven
Hallowed be thy name.
Thy Kingdom come,
Thy will be done
On earth as it is in heaven.
Give us this day our daily bread and
Forgive us our trespasses
As we forgive those
Who trespass against us.
Lead us not into temptation,
But deliver us from evil. ✝

Morning, Noon and Night

The Lord's Prayer (modern)

OUR FATHER in heaven,
Hallowed be your name.
Your kingdom come,
Your will be done,
On earth as in heaven.
Give us today our daily bread.
Forgive us our sins
As we forgive those
Who sin against us.
Save us from the time of trial
And deliver us from evil. †

Doxology

GLORY BE to the Father,
And to the Son
And to the Holy Spirit,
As it was in the beginning,
Is now and ever shall be,
World without end. †

Morning, Noon and Night

Hail Mary

HAIL MARY, full of grace, the Lord is with thee. Blessed art thou among women and blessed is the fruit of thy womb, Jesus. Holy Mary, Mother of God, pray for us sinners, now and at the hour of our death. †

Memorare

REMEMBER, O most gracious virgin Mary that never was it known that anyone who fled to your protection, implored your help or sought your intercession was left unaided. Inspired by this confidence I fly unto you, O virgin of virgins my mother, to thee do I come, before thee I stand sinful and sorrowful. O mother of the Word Incarnate, despise not my petition, but in your mercy hear and answer me. †

Morning, Noon and Night

The Apostles' Creed

I BELIEVE in God, the Father Almighty, Creator of heaven and earth; and in Jesus Christ, his only Son, Our Lord, who was conceived by the Holy Spirit, born of the Virgin Mary, suffered under Pontius Pilate,
was crucified, died and was buried.
He descended into hell, the third day he rose again from the dead.
He ascended into heaven and sits at the right hand of the Father Almighty.
From thence he shall come to judge the living and the dead.
I believe in the Holy Spirit,
the holy Catholic Church,
the Communion of Saints,
the forgiveness of sins,
the resurrection of the body,
and life everlasting. ✝

Morning, Noon and Night

Anima Christi

SOUL of Christ, sanctify me.
Body of Christ, save me.
Blood of Christ, fill me.
Water from the side of Christ, wash me.
Passion of Christ, strengthen me.
O good Jesus, hear me.
Within your wounds hide me.
Never let me be parted from you.
From the malicious enemy defend me.
In the hour of my death call me
And bid me come to you
That with your saints I may
praise you forever and ever. †

Morning, Noon and Night

Workers' Prayer

GOD, SEND US into our work this week with new resolves. Help us to solve the problems that have perplexed us and to serve the people we meet. May we see our work as part of your great plan and find satisfaction in what we do. We do not know what any day will bring to us, but we do know the hour for serving you is always present. We dedicate our hearts, minds and wills to your glory, through Christ our Lord. †

Morning, Noon and Night

Prayer of St. Francis

LORD MAKE me an instrument of your peace. Where there is hatred, let me sow love; where there is injury, pardon; where there is doubt, faith; where there is despair, hope; where there is darkness, light; and where there is sadness, joy.

Divine Master, grant that I may not so much seek to be consoled as to console; to be understood as to understand; to be loved as to love.

For it is in giving that we receive; it is in pardoning that we are pardoned; and it is in dying that we are born to eternal life. ✝

Morning, Noon and Night

LORD JESUS CHRIST,
you gave me this day and I have
tried to live it as your disciple.
Send your Spirit upon me now
as I reflect on my day.
Help me recall your presence and
to remember those moments when I
responded faithfully to you as well as the
times I failed to do so.
Grant me the comfort of your mercy and
the courage to face the truth.
Help me most of all to put this day
behind me, to rest in your abiding love
and to go forward in confidence that you
will never leave me. †

Mark Neilsen

Bless The Lord, O My Soul
Prayers of Praise, Joy and Thanksgiving

Bless The Lord, O My Soul

Psalm 8

HOW BEAUTIFUL
your name, O God!
Praise in the heavens!
Praise on the lips of children!
Your goodness resounds
throughout the earth,
silencing your foes.

When I study the heavens,
when I see how you have shaped
moon and stars fixing them in space,
I know how small I am;
I wonder at your love.

Yet you have made us
little less than gods,
sharing with us your splendor,
making us caretakers
of your creation—
guardians of sheep and cattle,

Bless The Lord, O My Soul

wild beasts and tame,
of birds in the sky
and fish in ocean depths.

God, our God,
how beautiful is your name,
throughout the earth. †

O TENDER Father
you gave me more,
much more than
I ever thought to ask for.
I realize that our human desires
can never really match
what you long to give us.
Thanks,
and thanks again, O Father,
for having granted my petitions,
and that which I never realized I
needed or petitioned. †
St. Catherine of Siena

Bless The Lord, O My Soul

FOR the songbird in the tree outside,
>I praise you, God.

For the sunlight streaming through the windows,
>I praise you, God.

For the blossoms on the apple tree
>I praise you, God.

For primroses, pansies, forget-me-nots and wildflowers,
>I praise you, God.

For sounds of hammer and saw, lawn mower and drill,
>I praise you, God.

For machines which whir and spin, wash and clean,
>I praise you, God.

For running water and electric power, for telephone lines and TV aerials,
>I praise you, God.

For the laughter of children and the wisdom of grownups,
>I praise you, God.

Bless The Lord, O My Soul

For the kindness of neighbors and
   letters in the mail,
        I praise you, God.
For dreams of possibility and faraway
   places,
        I praise you, God.
For symphonies and lullabies, for
   poetry and nursery rhymes
   for fireworks and festivals,
        I praise you, God.
For family and friends, and
   for the gift of myself,
        I praise you, God.
And for everything else I hold in my
   heart—people, creatures and things
   too numerous to name,
        I give you thanks and praise,
        O loving God. †
                Elizabeth-Anne Vanek

Bless The Lord, O My Soul

BLESS THE LORD, O my soul!
Blessed art thou, O Lord.
Bless the Lord, O my soul,
and all that is within me
bless his holy name!

Bless the Lord, O my soul
and forget not all his benefits.
The Lord is compassionate and merciful
long-suff'ring and of great goodness.
He forgives all your iniquities
and heals all your diseases.

Bless the Lord, O my soul!
Blessed art thou, O Lord.
Bless the Lord, O my soul,
and all that is within me
bless his holy name! †

Greek Chant

Bless The Lord, O My Soul

WHEN I look back on my life,
O God, I see how you have
walked with me the whole way.
Though I didn't always trust you,
though I didn't always believe
you were with me, still you were
there, guiding and comforting me.
Today I praise and thank you
for your faithfulness, today I ask you
to continue this journey with me.
Wipe away my tears, steady my feet
and set me firmly on your path. †
Elizabeth-Anne Vanek

Bless The Lord, O My Soul

Psalm 67

LOOK upon us kindly, O God.
Bless us.
Let your face shine upon us.
Then will the earth know you;
then will the nations see your power.

All you nations, praise God!
All you nations, sing for joy!
God rules with justice,
guiding all peoples.

All you nations, praise God!
All you nations, sing for joy!

The earth yields its harvest—
blessings from our God.
Look upon us kindly, O God.
May the whole world give praise. †

Bless The Lord, O My Soul

WE THANK YOU, Lord of all creation, for the wonder of the world in which we live, for the earth and all that springs from it, and for the mystery of life and growth. We pray that our gratitude may be shown by our care to conserve the powers of the soil, by our readiness to learn from scientific research, and by our concern for a fair distribution of the earth's resources. We ask these things in the name of Christ the Lord. †

Basil Naylor

Bless The Lord, O My Soul

WE THANK YOU, God,
for the saints of all ages,
for those who in times of darkness kept
the lamp of faith burning,
for the great souls who saw
visions of larger truths
and dared to declare them,
for the multitude of quiet, gracious
souls whose presence purified and
sanctified the world; and for
those known and loved by us,
who have passed from this earthly
fellowship into the fuller life with you.
Accept this, our thanksgiving, through
Jesus Christ, to whom be praise and
dominion forever. †

Fellowship Litanies

Bless The Lord, O My Soul

Psalm 19

YOUR GLORY spans the heavens,
O God.
Each day, each night,
teaches the next;
silently, wordlessly,
your wonders fill the universe,
rousing the sun from its tent,
challenging it to the marathon.

And the sun runs its fiery course
across the skies
like a groom in search of his bride.

How right are your laws, O God;
they are life and wisdom,
truth and joy.
They reveal your goodness.

Your path is firm, unchanging;
your justice is finest gold,

Bless The Lord, O My Soul

sweeter than honey from the comb.

Your word forms me
and gives me life.
If I stray,
if I am blind to my faults,
wash away my sin.
Save me from pride,
free me from wickedness.

I speak from my heart;
may my words please you, O God,
my refuge. †

W E PRAISE YOU, Lord, for the strange and the silly.
For supernovas and odd-shaped animals. For the whimsical shape of a cloud, and the toothless grin of a baby.
For prisms, caves, and sneezes.
You have brightened our days with the gifts of wonder and mirth.

Bless The Lord, O My Soul

Through the work of your hands,
we are invited to giggle and gawk,
to stand wide-eyed and speechless
before the dance of creation. †
Nancy Summers

THANK YOU, GOD, for the gift
of faith that comes to us through
your Holy Word and through the faith
of our friends, family and Church.
Thank you for the gifts of Baptism
and the life of Christ it gave us.
Thank you most of all for the quiet voice
of assurance you place deep in our
hearts when we most need to hear it.
Help us to remember always that faith
is your gift to us and nothing we will
ever earn for ourselves. †
Mark Neilsen

Bless The Lord, O My Soul

O LORD, God of Being, giver of all
good gifts, I praise you for all the
wonders you have shown me.
Your mighty hand has both
given me life and sustained me
through all adversity.
You have given me all my loved ones
and the beauty of the world.
I thank you, my God,
for these marvels so far beyond my
feeble ability to understand.
If the gifts are this wonderful, how
much more so the Giver! †

Jean Royer

Bless The Lord, O My Soul

The Divine Praises

BLESSED be God.
Blessed be his holy name.
Blessed be Jesus Christ,
true God and true man.
Blessed be the name of Jesus.
Blessed be his most Sacred Heart.
Blessed be his most Precious Blood.
Blessed be Jesus in the most
Holy Sacrament of the altar.
Blessed be the Holy Spirit,
the Paraclete.
Blessed be the great Mother of God,
Mary most holy.
Blessed be her holy and
Immaculate Conception.
Blessed be her glorious Assumption.
Blessed be the name of Mary,
Virgin and Mother.
Blessed be St. Joseph,
her most chaste spouse.

Bless The Lord, O My Soul

Blessed be God in his angels
and in his saints. †

MOST HOLY TRINITY, we praise and thank you for revealing to us your Divine Image.
We praise and thank you for being Father, for creating us and staying with us to guide and nurture the faith of your people.
We praise and thank you for being Son, for becoming one of us in everything but sin and for suffering along with us to show us the depth of your love.
We praise and thank you for being Spirit, for touching our hearts with joy and courage, even in the face of death.
And we praise and thank you for being much more
than we can ever understand. †

Mark Neilsen

Bless The Lord, O My Soul

Magnificat

MY SOUL proclaims the greatness of the Lord, my spirit exalts in God my savior. For God has looked upon his handmaid's lowliness, and my name will be blessed forever. The Mighty One has done great things for me,
and holy is his name. His mercy is from age to age to those who fear him.
He has shown might with his arm, dispersing the arrogant of mind and heart. He has thrown down the mighty from their thrones but lifted up the lowly. The hungry he has filled with good things, the rich he has sent away empty. He has helped Israel his servant, remembering his mercy, according to his promise to our ancestors, to Abraham and to his descendants forever. †

Luke 1:46-55

My Hope Is In You, My God
Prayers of Hope and Trust in Times of Doubt

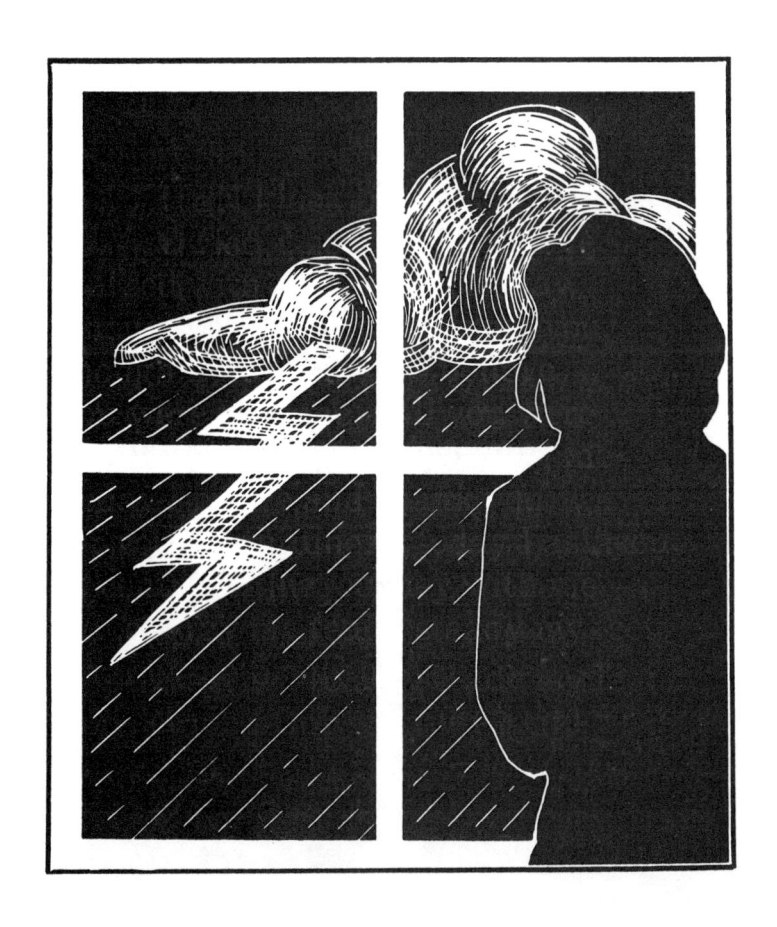

My Hope Is In You, My God

Psalm 11

IN YOU I take shelter, O my God.
People tell me to fly to the mountains
like a frightened bird.
"See how the wicked take
aim," they say.
"See them crouch in the shadows,
bows bent, arrows fixed, ready to cut
you down. When things fall apart,
what can you do about it?"

But you are in your temple, God.
Looking down from the heavens,
you hold the world in your gaze;
you search the hearts of humankind,
noting those who love and
those who hate.
You hurl your rage against the wicked,
scorching them with anger.
For you, God, love justice;
I will live to see your face. †

My Hope Is In You, My God

FATHER,
I abandon myself into your hands;
do with me what you will.
Whatever you may do I thank you:
I am ready for all, I accept all.

Let only your will be done in me,
and in all your creatures.
I wish no more that this, O Lord.

Into your hands I commend my soul:
I offer it to you
with all the love of my heart,
for I love you, Lord,
and so need to give myself,
to surrender myself into your hands,
without reserve,
and with boundless confidence,
for you are my Father. †

Charles de Foucauld

My Hope Is In You, My God

MY LORD GOD, I have no idea
where I am going.
I do not see the road ahead of me.
I cannot know for certain
where it will end.
Nor do I really know myself,
and the fact that I think
that I am following
your will does not mean
that I am actually doing so.
But I believe that the desire
to please you does in fact please you.
And I hope that I have that desire
in all that I am doing.
I hope that I will never do anything
apart from that desire.
And I know that if I do this,
you will lead me by the right road
though I may know nothing about it.
Therefore will I trust you always
though I may seem lost and in the
shadow of death.

My Hope Is In You, My God

I will not fear, for you are ever with me,
and you will not leave me
to face my perils alone. †
Thomas Merton

THERE WAS a time—O God, do you remember it?—when I wanted answers straight away.
There was a time when I looked for signs and tried to make bargains with you, thinking I could influence you in my favor.
Now I know that all time belongs to you and that your ways are not my ways.
Now I know that what you want is my love, not sacrifices.
I believe in you, God, I trust you know what is best for me.
Willingly, I put myself in your hands. †
Elizabeth-Anne Vanek

My Hope Is In You, My God

Psalm 16

KEEP ME, my God, for
you are my safety,
my only happiness.
I delight in fidelity;
those who choose other gods
bring troubles upon themselves.
When they pour out blood offerings
and praise the names of idols,
I will not join them.

You, God, are all I have;
everything depends on you.
You mark out for me
a place of beauty, my birthright.

You guide me;
you teach my heart, O God.
I will bless you.
I will think of you always,
mindful of your presence,

My Hope Is In You, My God

O God my strength.

I am filled with joy;
spirit and flesh exult.
You will not abandon me
or leave me among the dead.
No. You will lead me to life,
to endless joy,
at your right hand, forever. †

Act of Hope

O MY GOD, relying on your almighty power and infinite mercy and promises, I hope to obtain pardon of my sins, the help of your grace, and life everlasting, through the merits of Jesus Christ, my Lord and Redeemer. †

My Hope Is In You, My God

Psalm 13

WHEN, God? When will you remember me?
Will you turn away your face forever?
How many nights and days
will my enemies have me in their grip?
Answer me, God! Now!

Give me your light
or I shall slip into
the darkness of death.
Give me your light
or my enemies will gloat,
sneering at my fall.
I trust you, God;
you are kind and merciful.
Let my heart rejoice.
Let me sing of your love. †

My Hope Is In You, My God

LORD, ONE OF US doesn't seem to care anymore, doesn't listen or touch or help. It's probably me, but I have to say that it seems like you!
We are so far apart, and silence sits in the chasm like a vulture.
Maybe I stopped believing in you, but it feels like you stopped believing in me.
There, I've said it.
If you turned your face upon me now, would there not be a fury so great as to suck the breath from my body?
Or would there be the etchings of weary concern, like a parent searching
through the night for a lost child?
I think I know—and I believe. †

Nancy Summers

My Hope Is In You, My God

NO ONE WILL know how dark
my nights are. No one understands
the weight of my heart.

I fret, I withdraw, I find life a burden,
an almost unbearable burden.
I wish I too could smile from my heart.
I too long for peace and for
strength and courage.
I dread being alone;
and I fear talking to others.
Both solitude and company hold their
special terrors.

My fantasies are frightening;
I dare not utter them.
I wonder: am I going crazy?
Oh God, what is happening to me?
What has happened to joy
and pleasure and hope
and the thrill of being
close to people?

My Hope Is In You, My God

How do I get out of this
frightening gloom,
this dark tunnel with no light in sight?

I need you now,
as I've never needed you.
I need to believe you are there.
No, I need to feel you close.
Faith seems too vague a word
and human assurances feel empty.
Can you fill my heart today,
and lift me out of the pit?
From my hidden dangers, save me!
From the night of my depression,
release me! Set me free!

Break through these walls,
for I feel like a frightened child.
Take me by the hand and lead me to the
light. Take away the demons of my
fantasy and the dark, nameless terrors
I dread. Turn my weeping into joy!

May this suffering teach me

My Hope Is In You, My God

compassion and tenderness,
and give me a listening heart.
May it soften me and make me gentle,
ever willing to forgive,
and slow to condemn.

In my struggles,
never allow me to lose faith in you;
never let me be separated
from your love.
Even in my darkest moments,
may the light of your face
shine upon me,
and bring me peace and comfort.
This I ask as your child,
as your frightened and
lonely child.

Come soon!
Wipe away my tears! Heal my heart!
Set me free!
In your will is my peace. †

Joe Mannath, S.D.B.

My Hope Is In You, My God

Psalm 10

WHERE ARE YOU, O God?
Why do you hide from us
in times of distress?
The wicked throttle the poor,
cruelly devouring them.

Scorning you, O God,
they brag of their schemes.
"There is no God," they say;
"No one will punish us."

They turn their backs on you,
scoffing at your law,
mocking their rivals.

"Nothing can shake us," they boast.
"Let everyone else be cursed!"

Lies and spitefulness
spew from their mouths;

My Hope Is In You, My God

they crouch in hidden places,
waiting to murder the innocent.

Like savage lions
lurking in the undergrowth,
they wait to pounce on the poor
and drag them off in nets.

They lie in ambush,
then cruelly snatch their victims,
sneering, "As if God cares!"

Where are you, God?
Why do you hide from us?
The wicked spurn you—
and you let them go free!

O the agony and the torment, God—
you've seen them.
Come, reach out to us,
you, our only help!

Come, O God, and smash wickedness.
Trample the fruits of evil.

My Hope Is In You, My God

Banish corruption from this earth.
You, God, rule forever.
You, God, listen to our laments.
You, our courage and justice.
You, our safety. †

WHY, O Lord, is it so hard for
me to keep my heart
directed toward you?
Why do the many little things I want to
do, and the many people I know, keep
crowding into my mind, even during the
hours that I am totally free to be with
you and you alone?
Why does my mind wander off in so
many directions, and why
does my heart desire the things
that lead me astray?
Are you not enough for me?
Do I keep doubting your love and care,
your mercy and grace?

My Hope Is In You, My God

Do I keep wondering, in the center of
my being, whether you will give me all I
need if I just keep my eyes on you?
   Please accept my distractions,
my fatigue, my irritations, and my
faithless wanderings.
You know me more deeply and fully
than I know myself.
You love me with a greater love than I
can love myself.
You even offer me more
than I can desire.
Look at me, see me in all my misery
and inner confusion, and
let me sense your presence
in the midst of my turmoil.
All I can do is show myself to you.
Yet, I am afraid to do so.
I am afraid that you will reject me.
But I know—with the knowledge of
faith—that you desire
to give me your love.
The only thing you ask of me is not to
hide from you, not to run away

My Hope Is In You, My God

in despair, not to act as if
you were a relentless despot.
Take my tired body, my confused
mind, and my restless soul into your
arms and give me rest,
simple quiet rest.
Do I ask too much too soon? I should not
worry about that.
You will let me know.
Come, Lord Jesus, come. †

Henri Nouwen

LORD GOD, trust and hope in your goodness is a gift my heart aches for, a gift only you can give.
Grant me this favor in your good time
and patience in the meanwhile.
Help me to accept your will for me
and my own powerlessness to gain
for myself what I most desire. †

Mark Neilsen

Fear Not, I Am With You
Prayers in Time of Illness

Fear Not, I Am With You

Psalm 91

YOU who shelter in God,
   secure in God's shadow,
say, "You are my strength!
I trust you!"

For God will save you
from the trapper's net,
hiding you,
shielding you with gentle wings.

Don't be afraid of night's terrors,
of plagues that stalk in darkness;
don't be afraid of speeding arrows
that pierce daylight with disaster.

Though thousands fall,
you will be safe;
God will shield you from harm.

Angel wings enfold you;

Fear Not, I Am With You

angel arms will carry you
over snakes and stones.
You will trample savage beasts.

Cling tightly and God will save you,
raising you high.
Call out in your distress
and God will answer you.
Safety and honor,
long life and happiness! †

O GOD, CREATOR of humankind,
I do not aspire to comprehend
you or your creation, nor to understand
pain or suffering. I aspire only to relieve
the pain and suffering of others,
and I trust in doing so,
I may understand more clearly
your nature, that you are the Father of
all humankind, and that the hairs of my
head are numbered. †

St. Francis of Assisi

Fear Not, I Am With You

LORD, I'M NOT used to being sick. Since this illness began, I have been very angry and impatient.
I thought I had all the answers.
I prayed for some specific cures, as if I knew exactly what was best for me. Well, I don't know all the answers.
But now I realize that I need your loving presence every moment more than I have ever needed it.
O God, I believe in you.
Help my unbelief. †
Sr. Marguerite Zralek, O.P.

LORD JESUS, you shared the life of an earthly home at Nazareth and visited the homes of your friends. Come into my home and touch me in this illness. Restore me to health and wholeness to the praise of your holy name. †
John Gunstone

Fear Not, I Am With You

LORD JESUS, you know
what pain is like.
You know the torture of the scourge upon
your back, the sting of thorns upon your
brow, the agony of the nails in your
hands. You know what
I'm going through just now.
Help me to bear my pain
gallantly, cheerfully and patiently.
And help me to remember that I will
never be tried above what I am able to
bear, and that you are with me, even in
this valley of the deep dark shadow.
In ev'ry pang that rends the heart,
The Man of Sorrows had a part;
He sympathizes with our grief
And to the suff'rer sends relief. †
William Barclay

Fear Not, I Am With You

WITH JOINED HANDS we come
   to you, Lord, to ask you to use
your power of healing
   to cure this illness we face.

We realize that illness is
an inevitable part of life
   which we must occasionally accept
      and learn to endure,
   but when it strikes we get so fed up
      and discouraged with it.

We often give in to complaining
      and feeling sorry for ourselves.

Comfort us, Lord, and teach us
   how to be patient with our illnesses.

Help us learn to regard them
   not as causes for discouragement
      and self-pity,
   but as opportunities for us to learn

Fear Not, I Am With You

to develop acceptance and endurance.

Grant us, dear Lord, not only the wisdom
but also the will and the
determination we need
to always cooperate wholeheartedly
with your healing power.

We have confidence, Lord,
that you will restore our strength
and guide us back to health.

Thank you, Lord, for always blessing us
with your comfort and healing. †
Renee Bartkowski

Fear Not, I Am With You

TEACH ME, Lord God, to offer my
body as a living sacrifice to you:
my head, my arms, my legs; my conscious and my unconscious—impulses,
thoughts, desires, ambitions—all
the known and unknown that
make up the real me.
Teach me, also, to offer those parts of
my body which are sick and disabled.
Cleanse me, heal me, and
renew me by your Spirit.
Through the offering of your beloved
Son on the cross of Calvary, may the
offering of my body be a spiritual act of
worship holy and pleasing to you. †
John Gunstone

Fear Not, I Am With You

For the Terminally Ill

GOD, YOU ARE the giver of life.
You know the length of our days,
the hidden frailty we carry with us.
You hold all things in your hands.
In your goodness, in your great mercy,
remember those who will die this day.
Remember those who are terminally ill:
ease their pain and their fears,
surround them with loving friends and
relatives. Remember, also, those who
will die in accidents or as a result of
natural disasters. And God remember
especially the victims of war and violence: be with them in their agony. Let
your grace ease their sufferings and fill
their hearts with your forgiveness. We
ask this in the name of Jesus, the
Crucified, whose dying and rising has
given us the pattern of our lives. †
Elizabeth-Anne Vanek

Fear Not, I Am With You

For the Chemically Dependent

GRACIOUS LORD,
the helper of all who trust in you
we pray particularly for those
  who are addicted to alcohol,
    tobacco and drugs.

Give them both the desire and the will
  to be freed from their slavery,
and pour upon them your grace
    and guidance,
  leading them to your liberty
    and salvation.

Grant us the patience and love
  to stand by them
    in compassion and encouragement
  as servants of your hope and strength.

Lord, hear us for them. †

John Gunstone

Fear Not, I Am With You

O LORD HELP ME believe that
behind the clouds there is the sun
even when it rains, help me believe
the barren trees of autumn
will bear new leaves again if I am
patient enough to wait.
O Lord, help me realize the only way to
reach a mountain is to accept to go
through the long valley, the only way a
candle can share its light is by
gradually dying to itself.
Dear Lord, teach me to let go of the
securities that make me insecure, teach
me to let go of the fears that make me
restless and impatient.
Yes, I am afraid because I am so
vulnerable. I get edgy and irritable. I
wish it would be different, but that's the
way it is. And after all, I am not
ashamed to feel the way I do because I
am the one stuck on this bed.
But this is your world, O Lord, not

Fear Not, I Am With You

mine. I am here to serve you and understand you and I need to trust the message of my imperfections.

I place myself into your arms just like a child who feels secure in his mother's arms. Help me trust what I cannot control, help me walk where I cannot see, help me believe that behind the clouds there is your rising sun. †
Arnaldo Pangrazzi, O.S. Cam.

O JESUS, YOU suffered and died for us; you understand suffering; teach me to understand my suffering as you do; to bear it in union with you; to offer it with you to atone for my sins and to bring your grace to souls in need. Calm my fears and increase my trust. May I gladly accept your holy will and become more like you in trial. If it be your holy will, restore me to health so that I may work for your honor and glory and the salvation of all. †

Fear Not, I Am With You

O LORD, SEND your peace and your blessing upon me to sustain me.
Every day you show your care for your creation by nourishing the lilies of the field and the birds of the air.
You give every bird its food even though you don't throw it into their nests.
Enable me, your special creature, to recognize your loving presence whenever you reach out to me in your word, in your people, in
the mystery of my life.
As I am now confronted with this sickness, I pray that you may bless the doctors, the nurses, the chaplains to whom you have entrusted
your ministry of healing. Make my body, mind and soul receptive to your healing so that I may receive strength where I need to be strengthened, new life where I am failing. †

Arnaldo Pangrazzi, O.S. Cam.

Fear Not, I Am With You

O LORD, MY SHEPHERD, I don't remember anymore the pain of yesterday, I don't know about the pain of tomorrow. But, please, help me handle and bear the pain of today.

Give me the human and spiritual strength I need to bear it. Help me remember your cross, your prayer to the Father, your attitude.

Free me from the tendency to feel sorry for myself, from my need to complain about things and people around me. I just don't appreciate long visits any more, or the efforts of friends to cheer me up.

So, Lord, even when it hurts inside, provide strength within me that I may not be a burden to others but rather a source of peace and courage.

Fear Not, I Am With You

Guide me to see your love made present
in the faces of people who care for me.
Help me discover in the voices that
break the silence of my day the comfort
and promise of a life renewed.
I ask this in Jesus' name. †
Arnaldo Pangrazzi, O.S. Cam.

WHERE THERE IS pain,
    God is present.
Where there is despair,
    hope is hidden.
Where there is oppression,
    freedom will rise.
Where there is hurt,
    healing waits.
Where there is conflict,
    peace shall again be born.
Where there is death,
    new life can grow.
If only we have eyes that can
    see in the dark. †
John D. Powers

For The Sake Of Others
Prayers of Intercession

For The Sake Of Others

Psalm 20

ON THE DAY of terror,
God will answer your cries.
God's name protect you!
God's holiness defend you!
May God remember your offerings,
your sacrifice,
satisfying the deepest longings of your heart,
giving you the victory.
Then will we shout for joy
and wave our banners.
May God hear you!

Now I know
that God has given you the prize.
Now I know
that God has given you the battle.
God's hand saves!

People rely on horses and chariots

For The Sake Of Others

but we call on the name of our God.
They will reel and stumble
while we stand firm.

God, mighty God,
answer us when we call. †

For the Struggling

REMEMBER, O God, all those who are struggling this day: those who are poor, hungry and unemployed; those who lack shelter; those whose work is physically and emotionally draining; those who are trapped by dead ends or oppressive situations; those who are the victims of violence. Remember, also, God, the sick, the dying and the imprisoned, as well as their families and friends. Reach out to them and comfort them. Let them taste
your kindness and your mercy. †
Elizabeth-Anne Vanek

For The Sake Of Others

For Families

GOD, OUR FATHER, loving and merciful, we pray for the needs of families: for abundant love, for forgiveness and reconciliation, for a living faith to face the challenges of each day. Jesus, you know what families need to nourish both children and parents in long-lasting bonds of loving service and mutual respect. Help families of all shapes and sizes turn to you as their source of life. Holy Spirit, encourage husbands and wives, mothers and fathers, brothers and sisters, and give them all the eyes to appreciate one another. Help us all to be grateful for the gift of families. †

Mark Neilsen

For The Sake Of Others

For the Sick

GOD OF ALL goodness and love, hear our prayers for the sick members of our community and for all who are in need. Amid mental and physical suffering may they find consolation in your healing presence. Show your mercy as you close wounds, cure illness, make broken bodies whole and free downcast spirits. May these special people find lasting health and deliverance, and join us in thanking you for all your gifts. We ask this through the Lord Jesus who healed those who believed. ✝

For The Sake Of Others
___

For the Mentally Ill

FATHER, we pray for
the mentally ill,
for all who are of a disturbed
and troubled mind. Be to them light in
their darkness, their refuge and their
strength in time of fear. Give special
skills and tender hearts to all who care
for them, and show them how best to
assist in your work of healing; through
Jesus Christ Our Lord. †
Timothy Dudley-Smith

For the Poor

O GOD, the refuge of the poor, the
strength of those who toil, and the
Comforter of all who sorrow, we commend to your mercy the unfortunate
and needy in whatever land they may

For The Sake Of Others

be. You alone know the number and extent of their sufferings and trials. Look down, Father of mercies, at those unhappy families suffering from war and slaughter, from hunger and disease, and other severe trials. Spare them, O Lord, for it is truly a time for mercy. †

St. Peter Canisius

For Justice and Peace

ALMIGHTY and eternal God, may your grace enkindle in all of us a love for the many unfortunate people whom poverty and misery reduce to a condition of life unworthy of human beings. Arouse in the hearts of your people a hunger and thirst for social justice and for fraternal charity in deeds and in truth. Grant, O Lord, peace in our days: peace to souls, peace to families, peace to our country and peace among nations. †

For The Sake Of Others

For Life

O GOD, OUR CREATOR, all life is in your hands from conception until death. Help us to cherish our children and to reverence the awesome privilege of our share in creation. May all people live and die in dignity and love. Bless all those who defend the rights of the unborn, the handicapped and the aged. Enlighten and be merciful toward those who fail to love, and give them peace. Let freedom be tempered by responsibility, integrity and morality. We ask all this in Jesus' name. †

For The Sake Of Others

For Our Enemies

JESUS, when you taught your disciples how to pray, you insisted they should pray for their enemies. Then, in your death agony, you forgave those who tortured you. By your words and your example, you call us to pray for those who have hurt us in any way.
The price of discipleship is high, Lord. Instinct tells us to strike back, to get even, and sometimes to outdo the pain inflicted on us.
You tell us not merely to forgive and forget, but to *remember* and forgive.
You tell us to love these enemies of ours while knowing and experiencing full well what they have done to us.
This is not easy, Lord.
Teach us the way of mercy that we may discover your forgiveness. †

Elizabeth-Anne Vanek

For The Sake Of Others

For World Leaders

LET US PRAY for those
in high positions in the world
and for all who are called to leadership,
that they may make
other people's lives secure
and that they do not yield
to the power of corruption and injustice,
but champion the cause of the poor
and the underprivileged.
Let us also pray
for all who are engaged in international
politics, that they may never cease in
their attempts to find peace
and that there may be an end
to the senseless destruction of
so many human lives. †

Huub Oosterhuis

For The Sake Of Others

For Courage for Ourselves

GIVE US courage, O Lord, to stand up and be counted, to stand up for those who cannot stand up for themselves, to stand up for ourselves when it is needed.
Let us fear nothing more than we fear you.
Let us love nothing more than we love you, for so we shall fear nothing also.
Let us have no other God before you, whether nation or
party or state or church.
Let us seek no other peace but yours, and make us its instruments,
opening our eyes, ears and our hearts, so that we should know always what work of peace we may do for you. †

Alan Paton

For The Sake Of Others

For Family Members Who Lack Faith

GOOD JESUS, look with compassion on my loved ones who are not able to believe in you right now. Ready them to accept the gift of faith. Let them know that the life you offer them is much sweeter than whatever they fear might be lost through belief in you. Give them eyes to see that
all they savor and value so highly in this life is just a small token of what you long to give each one of us. Lord, please help all believers to become faithful, living signs of your love.
I believe you accept my concern for these dear ones, for you are the Good Shepherd who seeks the lost with more passion than I could ever imagine.
Mark Neilsen

For The Sake Of Others

For the Church

JESUS, AT THE Last Supper you prayed that all those who believed in you would be one. Today we are divided, Lord. We have our separate rituals and dogmas, rules and traditions. We call ourselves Christians and yet we remain separate from one another. Break down all barriers, Lord. Help us to see your saving presence among us. Help us to find unity in the bread we break and the wine we drink. Bring us together, Lord, in the mystery of your love. †
Elizabeth-Anne Vanek

WE PRAY YOU, Lord, to direct and guide your Church with your unfailing care, that it may be vigilant in times of quiet, and daring in times of trouble, through Jesus Christ our Lord. †
Franciscan Breviary

For The Sake Of Others

For the Pope

GOOD SHEPHERD, we pray for your protection and guidance over our Holy Father. Give him strength and wisdom to stand as a prophet for our times. May he be a light in darkness around which we gather in hope. We ask you to bring about reconciliation through his faithful teaching of peace and justice. Grant him compassion and care to live the gospel in love and service to all people. Let him follow in the path of Peter and Paul who, filled with the Holy Spirit, preached that the Lord saves all who call upon his name. †

For Vocations

LORD OF THE HARVEST, your Word finds a home in our hearts, calls us into community and invites us

For The Sake Of Others

to generous service of the human
family. Bless with courage and spirit
your priestly people, called to full
participation in the one Body of Christ.
May many choose to respond in
public service to your call offered
in Jesus' name. †
Cardinal Joseph L. Bernardin

For All Who Serve the Church

LORD JESUS, you touch the men
and women of the world through the
faithful ministry of your Church.
May all who have the responsibility of
serving in and through the Church be
granted the wisdom and love they need
to bring your message to the world.
May all bishops and priests be faithful
teachers and guides, and may all who
minister in your name serve your
people in fidelity, humility and joy. †
Mark Neilsen

Forgive Me, I Have Sinned
Prayers of Penitence

Forgive Me, I Have Sinned

Psalm 51

GOD of all mercy
in your goodness,
in your great tenderness,
have pity on me.
Wipe away my faults, my guilt;
wash me clean.

For I turned against you,
hardening my heart,
flaunting my evil ways.
Now sin weighs heavily upon me;
I know what I have done.

How right your judgment!
My own sins condemn me.
You saw my guilt,
even before I was born.

Ground me now in your truth;
center me in your wisdom.

Forgive Me, I Have Sinned

Scrub me, scour me
until I am as pure
as falling snow.

God, give me a new heart,
a steady spirit.
Do not reject me,
leaving me orphaned.

Save me, be my joy,
give me a willing heart.
Then I will teach sinners
and they will turn to you.

Save me
and I will sing of your mercy.
Give me words of praise
and I will sing.

It is not a holocaust
that you want
but a contrite heart.
I offer you my tears,
my shattered spirit.

Forgive Me, I Have Sinned

Loving God, tender God,
accept this gift;
recreate me in your image
that I may live. †

YOU did not come, O God,
to judge us
but to seek what is lost,
to set free those
who are imprisoned in guilt and fear
and to save us
when our hearts accuse us.
Take us as we are here,
with all that sinful past
of the world.
You are greater than our heart
and greater than all our guilt—
you are the creator
of a new future
and a God of love
for ever and ever. †

Huub Oosterhuis

Forgive Me, I Have Sinned

Act of Contrition

O MY GOD, I am heartily sorry for having offended you.
I detest all my sins because
of your just punishments,
but most of all,
because they offend you, my God,
who are all good and
deserving of all my love.
I firmly resolve with the help of your grace to sin no more and to avoid the near occasions of sin. ✝

Forgive Me, I Have Sinned

Prayer Before Reconciliation

DEAR GOD, I have come here to acknowledge my sinfulness and to ask your forgiveness.
Help me to see myself as you see me—to see not only my faults but also my goodness, to see not only when I have strayed, but also when I have been faithful to your call. Let me see things as they are, clearly and objectively, so that I may name my weakness without growing discouraged. †

Elizabeth-Anne Vanek

The Jesus Prayer

LORD JESUS Christ,
Son of the living God,
have mercy on me, a sinner. †

(It is an Eastern Christian tradition to repeat these words continuously to invoke in our hearts the healing power of Jesus' name.)

Forgive Me, I Have Sinned

DEAR GOD, for the many times I have knowingly done what is wrong in your sight, I am sorry.
For the many more times I have resisted doing what is right, sometimes even refusing to look directly at a situation just so I wouldn't have to make a hard decision, I am sorry.
For the times I feel so weak I seem unable to acknowledge evil and ask for your help, I am sorry.
Help me to trust in you enough that I can ask your assistance in times of temptation.
Help me to hope in your mercy, in good times and in bad times.
Help me, even in the most confusing situations, to find the way to love you, to love myself and to love others. †

Mark Neilsen

Forgive Me, I Have Sinned

DEAR JESUS, you know me as I really am. You know the faults I try to keep hidden, even from myself. Help me to recognize, as the Good Thief did, that I have done wrong and deserve punishment. Give me the courage to accept myself as I am and to depend on your mercy as my only hope of forgiveness and new life. †

LORD OF HEAVEN and Earth, I know I stand in need not only of your forgiveness but also the forgiveness of those I have hurt. I ask you to accept my prayer and move their hearts that they also might forgive me. I know this may not be easy or swift, so I ask for the gift of patience as I wait for the healing of these relationships. Help me to feel sincere sorrow and to change my life to avoid hurting people in this way. †

Forgive Me, I Have Sinned

Psalm 65

ALL PRAISE to you, loving God.
We give thanks
for you hear our prayers.

We come to you
clad in sin,
weighed down by faults
but you blot them away.

You invite us into your house,
filling us with good things,
repaying us with joy.

You are the hope of far-off lands
and distant isles,
the strength of mountains
and raging seas.
You hold all things in steadiness;
you still the roaring waves,
the din of war.

Forgive Me, I Have Sinned

Everyone wonders at your deeds.
From sunrise to sunset,
shouts of gladness!

You water the earth
and it teems with life.
You drench furrows,
break clods and bless tender shoots.
A rich harvest from our God!

Your goodness overflows
into deserts and hillsides,
meadows and valleys.
Grass thickens, wheat ripens,
flocks grow fat.

All is laughter
and dancing and song!
All is clothed in your beauty! †

Forgive Me, I Have Sinned

I CONFESS TO Almighty God,
and to you, my brothers and sisters,
that I have sinned
through my own fault,
in my thoughts and in my words,
in what I have done and
what I have failed to do;
and I ask blessed Mary, ever virgin,
all the angels and saints,
and you, my brothers and sisters,
to pray for me to the Lord our God.✝

Roman Rite

Dwelling As One
Prayers for the Family

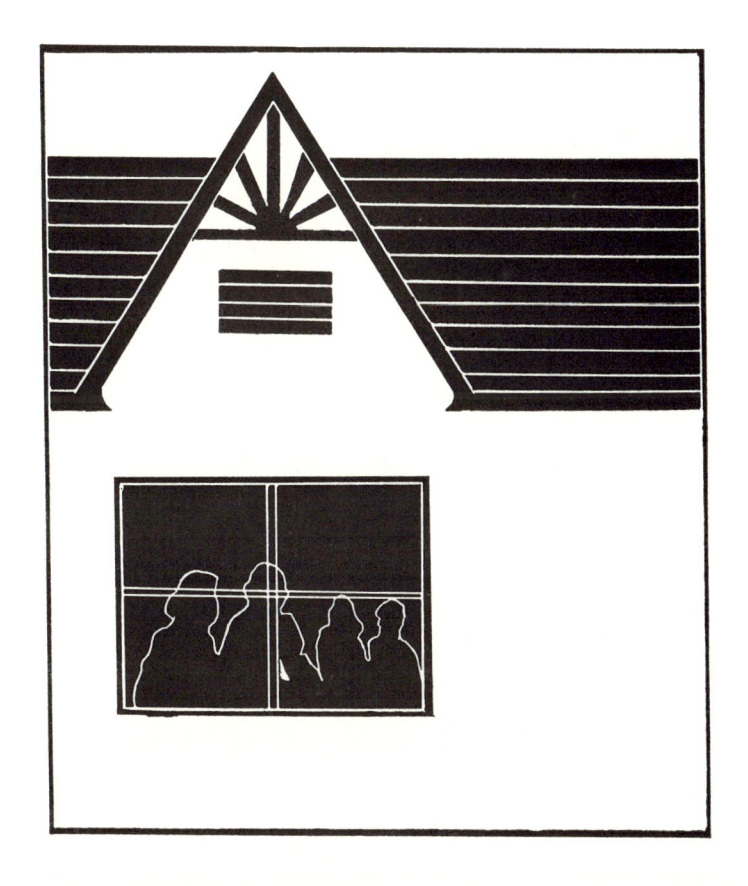

Dwelling As One

Psalm 84

I LOVE your house, O God.
How I yearn for your courts!
My spirit, my flesh,
ache with longing,
O God, my life.

Even the sparrow finds a home,
even the swallow builds a nest
for its young,
near the altar,
O God, my God.

So happy to live in your house!
So happy to hide in your shelter,
to praise you, day and night!

You are strength for the journey,
courage for the way.
Spring rains water the valleys
as pilgrims climb from height to height,

Dwelling As One

seeking your holy place.

God, God my life,
hear me.
Listen, God of Jacob,
God our shield.
Look kindly upon your anointed one.
One day, one day in your house, O God,
is better than a thousand days
anywhere else;
even your doorstep is better
than the lodgings of the wicked.

For you are sun and shelter,
grace and glory.
You give good things
to those who walk in your truth.
God, God my life,
how happy those who trust in you! †

Dwelling As One

BLESS OUR HOME, Lord,
and fill it with your love
 and your presence.

We ask you to come and dwell within its walls—
 to live in the midst of us
  and help make our home
  a special place
   where we can nurture each other
   and help each other grow.

Dear Lord, join us in our effort
 to make our home a warm
  and secure haven
 where we can come to renew our
  energies
  and refresh our spirits.

Help us make it a refuge
 where anxieties are relieved,
  laughter is shared,

Dwelling As One

and love is dispensed freely and
 generously.

Let our home be a place where the door
 is always open
  so we can offer friendship,
  solace, and joy
 to friends and relatives,
  to lonely and needy people.

Help make it a place where those who
 enter can find
  a shoulder to lean on,
  a hand to hold,
  and arms to embrace them.

Lord, let this home of ours
 always be a special sanctuary
  where we can feel your presence
  and where we can receive
  your love. †

Renee Bartkowski

Dwelling As One

WE THANK you, Father,
for the gift of Jesus your Son
who came to our earth and lived in a
simple home. We have a greater
appreciation of the value and
dignity of the human family
because he loved and was loved
within its shelter.
Bless us this day; may we grow in love
for each other in our family and
so give thanks to you who are the
maker of all human families and
our abiding peace. †

Michael Buckley

Dwelling As One

For Our Family

I BRING to you our little family
with all our hopes and dreams.

You know what we need better
than we do. You love us far more
than we can love each other.

Each one of us is a gift of your love,
a gift to our family, a gift to the world.

Of all the wondrous ways in which
you speak to me,
the first and the deepest,
the happiest and the hardest,
is the voice of my family.
I would not be what I am today
except for my dear ones.

Thank you for my family.
Thank you for everything we share.

Dwelling As One

Thank you for joy and laughter and
tears and work,
and for the unique gifts
each of us brings.
Thank you, above all, for the gift of love
which makes this our home—
a love we breathed and
touched and knew
before we ever heard the word.
Thank you for this opportunity
to celebrate your love for us.

Pardon us and heal us,
for we hurt each other.
Forgive us our lack of love,
our selfish withdrawal,
and words, deeds and silences that
wound the heart.
We need your healing every day, every
hour, every moment.
Without your constant care,
how could we hold each other in love?

Source of all love, make us aglow

Dwelling As One

with love.
Make us thoughtful and caring,
generous in forgiving,
joyful in service,
open to give and to receive.

May our love and unity
open our hearts to you,
and to the great human family
to which we belong.

May all families everywhere
know true love, peace and security.
May every family be
a powerhouse of love,
a source of healing,
a place of joy.

And may we treat one another,
always and everywhere,
as members of your one great family. †
Joe Mannath, S.D.B.

Dwelling As One

LORD GOD, from you every family in heaven and on earth takes its name. Father, you are Love and Life.

Through your Son, Jesus Christ, born of woman, and through the Holy Spirit, the fountain of divine charity, grant that every family on earth may become for each successive generation a true shrine of life and love.

Grant that your grace may guide the thoughts and actions of husbands and wives for the good of their families and of all the families in the world.

Grant that the young may find in the family solid support for their human dignity and for their growth in truth and love.

Grant that love, strengthened by the grace of the sacrament of marriage, may prove mightier than all the weaknesses and trials through which our families sometimes pass.

Dwelling As One

Through the intercession of the Holy Family of Nazareth, grant that the Church may fruitfully carry out her worldwide mission in the family and through the family.
We ask this of you, who are Life, Truth and Love with the Son and Holy Spirit. †

Pope John Paul II

WHEN THINGS GO wrong for one of us, God, very often everyone suffers. Tension mounts, harsh words are said, feelings are hurt. Help us not to take out our frustrations on each other. Help us to be understanding and forgiving. Help us to remember that you are with us in our struggles, however difficult they may seem. And give us the wisdom not to go to bed before settling our differences. †

Elizabeth-Anne Vanek

Dwelling As One

For Children, Grown and Gone

LORD JESUS, I can still remember when they filled the house. I remember when they were babies, and I remember when they were teenagers. I remember when I shouted at them and scolded, and I remember times when they were angry with me. I remember, too, how my heart ached with love for them, as it still does today. Thank you for my children, now living lives of their own. Be with them, Jesus, and give them your Holy Spirit in abundant measure, to guard and guide them. Send your angels to protect them, and may our Blessed Mother watch over them. Keep them close to you, O Lord, even if I may not understand your ways of doing that. Thank you again, Lord, for my children, grown and gone. †

Mitch Finley

Dwelling As One

For Mothers

ALMIGHTY GOD, you became human through a woman and you know well what it takes to be a mother. Give all mothers the courage they need to face the uncertain future that the presence of children always brings. Give them the strength to love and to be loved in return, not perfectly, but humanly. Give them the faithful support of husband, family and friends as they take each step with their children. Most of all, give them the willingness to turn to you for help when they need it most. †

Dwelling As One

For Fathers

OUR FATHER in heaven, you have promised always to be with us to strengthen, guide and sustain us in your way. Grant the fathers of this world the same determination to strengthen, guide and sustain their own children. Help them to love tenderly, to discipline firmly and to accept warmly the children with which you have blessed them. Give them the loving support of wife, family and friends as they give their special gifts of fidelity and love to their children and to the world. †

Dwelling As One

OUR WORLD gets so small at times, Lord.
We often get so wrapped up in our own
   comfort and welfare
      that we forget about the world
      outside our door—
   the world of poverty
      and famine
      and disease
      and war—
   the world of people suffering,
      lacking homes,
      lonely.

We don't ever want to get so involved
   in our own interests
      that we forget to be our
      brothers' and sisters' keepers.

Don't let us ever get so obsessed
   with our own success and happiness
      that we forget that we have a

Dwelling As One

    share in making life easier and
      happier for those who are
      less fortunate than we are.

Let us always remember, Lord,
    that we are *all* responsible
      for making this world
      a better place . . .
      not only for our children
but for the children
    of our neighbors
    and the children of the world.

Help us always accept
    this responsibility
      willingly and eagerly. †

                    Renee Bartkowski

I Am The Life
Prayers of Mourning

I Am The Life

Psalm 23

LOVING GOD,
you shepherd me.

You lead me to green pastures
and quiet waters
where I can rest, renewed.

Even in the darkest valleys,
I fear nothing.
You are there beside me,
comforting me with your crook
and your staff.

Under my enemies' glare,
you set a feast for me;
you anoint my head with oil;
my cup overflows.

Your love overshadows me all my days.
Forever I will live in your house. †

I Am The Life

ACCEPT THESE TEARS as my prayer. Watch with me, please, and give me strength!

I have no words to tell you what I feel.
You need no words to hear my cry.
Be with me, please, and hold my hand,
for I feel frightened and alone.

I knew, of course,
that death would part us one day.
But when the hour did come,
what a wrench it was!
A part of me died
and was buried with _____ .
I feel like a shadow of what I was before.

Receive my _____
into your loving embrace.
Someone I loved much, but in
my own poor way,
is certainly better off with you.

I Am The Life

I could not give him/her
all that he/she yearned for;
you can.
Help me to accept this truth,
and to rejoice in it.

I believe—I try to tell myself—
that death is not the end,
but a passage—
a passage to unspeakable glory
and life without end.
But I—I cannot see that or grasp it.
I am only human;
I am in pain and alone.
I can only see up to this door,
not the light that shines beyond it.

So, while I hope, while I trust,
while I accept your will,
strengthen my faith and give me courage.

I thank you for the love we have given
each other. I ask your pardon for the
hurts we have caused.

I Am The Life

I accept all—life, death, eternity—
as undeserved gifts from your mercy.

Throw your arms around me,
and comfort me!
See my tears! Hear my cry!
Turn my pain into hope,
my loneliness into wisdom, and my fear
into new strength for the new day.

May this death teach me
to prepare for my death,
and to pass my days in loving gratitude.
All that you do for us is love,
even when we do not understand it.
I do not seek to understand.
I ask for hope, for strength, for serenity.

Accept these tears; they are
all I have now.
Bless me! Give me hope! Out of my
mourning, bring new life for me and for
those I love. †

Joe Mannath, S.D.B.

I Am The Life

FATHER, GOD of all consolation,
in your unending love and mercy
for us you turn the darkness of death
into the dawn of new life.
Show compassion to your people
in their sorrow.
Be our refuge and our strength to lift us
from the darkness of this grief to the
peace and light of your presence.
Your Son, our Lord Jesus Christ, by
dying for us, conquered death
and by rising again, restored life.
May we go forward eagerly to meet him,
and after our life on earth be reunited
with our brothers and sisters where
every tear will be wiped away.
We ask this through Christ our Lord. †
Catholic Burial Rite

I Am The Life

RECEIVE, LORD, in tranquillity and peace, the souls of your servants who have departed out of this present life to be with you. Give them the life that knows no age, the good things that do not pass away; through Jesus Christ our Lord. †
St. Ignatius Loyola

GRANT, O LORD, to all who are bereaved the spirit of faith and courage, that they may have strength to meet the days to come with steadfastness and patience; not sorrowing as those without hope, but in thankful remembrance of your great goodness and in the joyful expectation of eternal life with those they love. And this we ask in the name of Jesus Christ our Savior. †
Gabe Huck

I Am The Life

O GOD, whose days are
without end and whose mercies
cannot be numbered: Make us deeply
aware of the shortness and uncertainty
of human life; and let your Holy Spirit
lead us in holiness and
righteousness all our days;
that, when we shall have
served you in our generation,
we may be gathered to our ancestors,
having the testimony of
a good conscience, in the communion
of the Church, in the confidence of
a certain faith, in the comfort of
a religious and holy hope,
in favor with you, our God, and
in perfect charity with the world.
All this we ask through
Jesus Christ our Lord. †

Gabe Huck

I Am The Life

For the Living and the Dead

LOVING GOD, Lord of all consolation, in fulfillment of your will,
Jesus conquered death and rose again,
that we might be saved. Hear our
prayers for our beloved dead whom
you have summoned to yourself.
They have died believing in Jesus
and are buried with him in the
hope of rising again.
We thank you for the fatherly care
you showed them in this life.
We ask you to forgive their sins,
that on the day of judgment they
may rise with all the saints to eternal
life and rest in your kingdom. Show
us also your mercy and compassion
because we miss them. Let our faith
be a comfort and assurance to one
another. May the Holy Spirit inspire
us to lives of holiness and justice in

I Am The Life

faithfulness to our baptism. Help us to remember that you alone know the day of our death. When your call comes, may we eagerly go to meet you and be reunited with our sisters and brothers. We hope for the peace of heaven where there will be no more sorrow or pain, and every tear will be wiped away. ✝

For Our Loved Ones in Purgatory

DEAR GOD, you alone know the faith of those you have called to yourself in death. In our love for them, we pray that you look upon them, and all the faithful departed, with your abundant mercy. Grant them eternal rest with you and all the saints of heaven. This we ask in the name of your Son, Jesus, who overcame death that we might live forever. ✝

I Am The Life

MAY THE ANGELS
lead you into paradise;
may the martyrs come to welcome you
and lead you into the the Holy City,
the new and eternal Jerusalem.
May the choir of angels welcome you,
and where Lazarus is poor no longer,
may you find eternal rest. †
Roman Funeral Rite

Christ Our Light
Prayers for the Church Year

Christ Our Light

Psalm 98

A NEW SONG!
Sing God a new song!
Praise for God's wonders,
for justice and saving power!
All nations have seen God's glory,
God's kindness and faithfulness
toward Israel.

Sing! Sing joyfully all you lands!
Break into song! Give praise!
Praise with trumpet and harp,
with the sound of the horn!
Sing! Sing joyfully!

All creatures of the earth and sea,
of rivers and mountains,
shout for joy!
God comes!
God comes to rule with justice.
A new song!
All the world give praise! †

Christ Our Light

An Advent Prayer

LOVING CREATOR of the Universe, we ask your help as we begin this season of joyful expectation. Give us the longing of your prophet Isaiah that our hearts might not settle for anything less than the coming of your reign. Give us the honesty of John the Baptist that we might know our need for repentance and forgiveness. And give us the courageous joy of Mary that we might become true disciples in spite of moments of uncertainty and sorrow. Lastly, dear God, give us patience that we might wait in hope for all your gifts to us. †

Mark Neilsen

Christ Our Light

As Christmas Approaches

LORD JESUS,
soon we will celebrate the wonder
of your birth.
Every time I glance at the tree
and look at the nativity set,
I am filled with the desire to just stop
and ponder the meaning of your coming.

Yet, Lord, I feel incapable
of inner peace and silence.
I run from store to store,
looking for bargains,
trying to stretch dollars—
which are becoming, by the way,
an extinct species here—
and neglecting all too often
the spirit of Advent.

Jesus Lord, you were ignored
when first you came to this planet.

Christ Our Light

And I wonder if you arrived today
as an Infant whether or not
we'd welcome you any more warmly.
I wonder if amid all our hustle and
bustle we'd have time to notice
the simplicity and humility
of a God willing to assume humanity
so that humanity could become more
God-like.

During a still night, you came—
heralded by the angels
and noticed only by the lowly
of this earth.
Help me Jesus, to be
like those shepherds.
I, too, have a "flock."
Let me look after them,
attend to their needs,
but never be so busy that I miss out
on your coming into my life.

Give me the patience and fortitude I
need to shop without resenting

Christ Our Light

people who are rude,
or who take the last
of the item I wanted,
or who pull into the parking space
I was eyeing.
Let me be inspired by your example:
there was no room for you at the inn,
yet you did not complain;
you were ignored by most people,
yet you did not resent this,
but considered humility and lowliness
the most regal of honors.

Give me, Lord, the grace I need
to explain the meaning of Christmas
to my children, who are surrounded
by the glare of the secular
and commercial.
Help me to understand their many
"wants," and to bear with
their seasonal tenseness.
Most of all, Lord,
enable me to make Christmas
a way of life,

a welcoming attitude that
always has room
for the spiritual
and always has time to give of self
for the good of others.

Come, Lord, into the world.
Come to this family in a special way.
Make us eager for your coming
and more worthy to receive you,
our Gift from the Father. †

Jeanie Gibson

Christmas

MAY Christmas find each of us engaged in rediscovering the message that comes from the manger in Bethlehem. A little courage is necessary, but it is worthwhile, because only if we can open out in this way to the coming of Christ, will we be able to experience the peace announced by the Angels during that holy night.

Christ Our Light

May Christmas be for you all a meeting
with Christ, who became human
to give everyone the capacity
of becoming a child of God. †
> *Pope John Paul II (adapted)*

LORD, HELP US look beneath the tinsel and the glitter of this season
and find you—not just a divine child
who makes us feel nostalgic
and sentimental, but you,
the living God, born into
pain and poverty, born into hatred and
rejection, born into a world of closed
doors and political intrigues.
As we remember your birth, O Jesus,
fill us with wonder at the mystery of
this love that sent you to us, show us
that Christmas is more
than a birthday party for children,
give us more than we bargained for
and find your way into our hearts. †
> *Elizabeth-Anne Vanek*

Christ Our Light

The Solemnity of Mary (New Year's Day)

LORD GOD, you have honored the
Blessed Virgin Mary for her
great and tender courage in
becoming the Mother of Jesus. We
remember her as we begin the new
year, remembering also our call
to become disciples in whose
hearts Jesus will dwell.
Grant us the grace to live our
baptismal promises more faithfully
in the coming year. Help us to face the
future with Mary's courage,
rooted as it was in
trust and prayer-filled hope.
May our year be touched by joy and
gratitude as we come to know and
follow you more completely. †

Mark Neilsen

Christ Our Light

Epiphany

DEAR JESUS, a star in the heavens drew three men from the east to your manger so long ago; let my heart be drawn to you now.
They knelt before you in homage; help me now to absorb some of the wonder of God become a tiny baby.
The wise men brought gifts of gold, incense and myrrh; grant me the generosity to give back some of what you have given me in service to others. Most of all, may the example of these three ancient seekers encourage me never to become willing to settle for less than your true presence. †

Christ Our Light

Lenten Psalm of Awakening

COME, O Life-giving Creator,
    and rattle the door latch
    of my slumbering heart.
Awaken me as you breathe upon
    a winter-wrapped earth,
    gently calling to life virgin Spring.

Awaken in these fortified days
    of Lenten prayer and discipline
    my youthful dream of holiness.
Call me forth from the prison camp
    of my numerous past defeats
    and my narrow patterns of being
    to make my ordinary life
        extra-ordinarily alive,
    through the passion of my love.

Show to me during these Lenten days
    how to take the daily things of life
    and by submerging them in the

Christ Our Light

sacred,
> to infuse them with a great love
> for you, O God, and for others.

Guide me to perform simple acts of love
> and prayer, the real works of
> reform and renewal
> of this overture to the spring of

the Spirit.

O Father of Jesus, Mother of Christ
> help me not to waste
> these precious Lenten days
> of my soul's spiritual springtime. †
>> *Edward Hays*

LORD JESUS CHRIST our Savior and Redeemer, I kneel before your blessed cross. I want to open my spirit and my heart to contemplate your holy sufferings. I want to place your cross before my poor soul that I might know a little better, receive more deeply into my own heart all that you did and

suffered, and that I might realize who it was for whom you suffered.
May your grace be with me, the grace to shake off the coldness of my heart, to forget my everyday life for at least a while, and to dwell with you in love, sorrow and gratitude. ✝
Karl Rahner, S.J.

Easter

LORD, IN THE GLORY of your rising, you bring all things to newness. In this season of great joy, wash away all pain, all ugliness, all sadness. Roll away all the stones and boulders that block our paths, trapping us with their weight. Untie all the shrouds and winding cloths that limit, bind and strangle hope. Call us from our tombs that we may find the music of possibility, the dance of grace and the rich, rich wine of your presence. ✝
Elizabeth-Anne Vanek

Christ Our Light

JESUS, YOUR disciples did not all immediately recognize your Risen Presence among them.
Help us now to have the eyes to see how you continue to bring new life among us. Give us the grace to be patient with ourselves when we can see only death and destruction, only pain and loss. Renew during this Easter Season our faith that we might believe in things unseen and hope in your promises of new life.
These things we ask as your disciples, who do not always recognize your Risen Presence among us. †

Mark Neilsen

Christ Our Light

Pentecost

COME, SPIRIT of God, transform your people with the fire of faith. Like your disciples gathered in the upper room, sometimes we need you to step through the doors we have locked against fear. Give light to our understanding that we may know your will for us. Grant us the courage to really mean it when we say, "Your will be done." Above all, kindle that flame within us that lets us know, beyond all questioning, that you have loved us into being, reclaimed us from the depths of sin and despair and prepared an everlasting home for those who follow your way on earth. Then we will sing your praise in word and deed all our days. †

Mark Neilsen

Christ Our Light

COME, HOLY SPIRIT, and from heaven direct on us the rays of your light. Come, Father of the poor; come, giver of God's gifts; come, light of the human heart.

Kindly Paraclete, in your gracious visits to the human soul you bring relief and consolation. If it is weary with toil, you bring it ease; in the heat of temptation, your grace cools it; if sorrowful, your words console it.

Light most blessed, shine on the hearts of your faithful—even into their darkest corners; for without your aid we can do nothing good, and everything is sinful.

Wash clean the sinful soul, rain down your grace on the parched soul and heal the injured soul. Soften the hard heart, cherish and warm the ice-cold heart,

Christ Our Light

and give direction to the wayward.

Give your seven holy gifts to your faithful, for their trust is in you. Give them reward for their virtuous acts; give them a death that ensures salvation; give them unending bliss. Amen. Alleluia. †
> *Adapted from the Sequence of the Mass of Pentecost*

Ordinary Time

WHEN THE FESTIVALS are over and the crowds have gone home, our life of faith gets back to normal. Sometimes that means the plodding dullness of duty as we struggle to do what we know we should even when we don't feel like it. Other times, moments of peace emerge in the commonplace and the daily grind is transfigured. God grant that we can be faithful to the ordinary that we might be made worthy

Christ Our Light

of the extraordinary love you reveal to us, day in and day out. In gratitude for that revelation and in hope for a deepening appreciation of the ordinary stuff of our lives, we pray in Jesus' name. †

Mark Neilsen

The Assumption of Our Lady

IMMACULATE VIRGIN, Mother of Jesus and our Mother, we believe in your triumphant assumption into heaven where the angels and saints acclaim you as Queen. We join them in praising you and bless the Lord who raised you above all creatures. With them we offer you our devotion and love. We are confident that you watch over our daily efforts and needs, and we take comfort from our faith in the coming resurrection. Intercede for us with your Son that we might live faithfully and enjoy eternal life. †

Christ the King

LORD JESUS CHRIST, you are the Ruler of all things in heaven and on earth. You who calmed the wind and waves when the seas raged, reign now in our hearts and grant us the peace of your kingdom. Help us put aside the idols and false gods that creep into our hearts; help us to follow the example of your Holy Mother Mary and give your life a place to grow within us. With the Church throughout the ages and all the angels and saints we join in saying:
All praise and honor and glory be yours forever and ever. †

Mark Neilsen

My God & My All

Special Devotions

My God & My All

To the Sacred Heart of Jesus

I FLY TO YOU, Sacred Heart of my Savior, for you are my refuge, my only hope. You are the remedy for all my miseries, my consolation in all my wretchedness, the reparation for all my infidelities, the supplement for all my deficiencies, the expiation for all my sins, the hope and the end of all my prayers. You are the only one who is never weary of me and who can bear with my faults, because you love me with an infinite love. Therefore, O my God, have mercy on me according to your great mercy, and do with me, and for me and in me whatever you will, for I give myself entirely to you, Divine Heart, with full confidence that you will never reject me. †

My God & My All

The Stations of the Cross

These Stations of the Cross are ideally used where stations have been erected for the purpose. Where physical stations are not available, one can pray before a crucifix and imagine following Jesus from station to station.

The brief meditations that accompany the stations here are offered only as guides to your own meditation or quiet prayer in the presence of the Passion and Death of Our Lord.

I. Jesus is Condemned to Death

We adore you, O Christ, and we praise you, because by your Holy Cross you have redeemed the world.

Jesus was sentenced to death, even though he was guilty of no transgression. The jealousy of the Jewish leaders and the cow-

My God & My All

ardice of the Roman authorities made him a victim. For our sake, he accepted their power over him.

Father, not my will but yours be done.

2. Jesus Takes Up His Cross

We adore you, O Christ, and we praise you, because by your Holy Cross you have redeemed the world.

Though exhausted from his beating at the hands of the Roman soldiers, Jesus was forced to carry the cross, the instrument of his own execution. He carried it as well as he could, giving an example to all who would follow him.

Father, not my will but yours be done.

3. Jesus Falls the First Time

We adore you, O Christ, and we praise you, because by your Holy Cross

My God & My All

you have redeemed the world.

The weight of the cross and the difficulty of the journey became too much for Jesus, and he fell. His willingness to accept an unjust death did not mean that it would be easy or over quickly. He pulled himself up, and continued on.

Father, not my will but yours be done.

4. Jesus Meets His Mother Mary

We adore you, O Christ and we praise you, because by your Holy Cross you have redeemed the world.

Jesus could no more protect Mary from the pain she suffered upon seeing him in torment than she could save him now. In a way, they bore one another's suffering, as all parents and children sometimes do.

My God & My All

Father, not my will but yours be done.

5. Simon of Cyrene Helps Jesus

We adore you, O Christ, and we praise you, because by your Holy Cross you have redeemed the world.

Worried that Jesus might not survive the arduous trip up to Calvary, the soldiers pressed Simon into helping him. Very likely Simon didn't recognize the great opportunity he had been given to cooperate in Jesus' saving mission.

Father, not my will but yours be done.

6. Veronica Wipes the Face of Jesus

We adore you, O Christ, and we praise you, because by your Holy Cross you have redeemed the world.

A woman traditionally called Veronica (meaning "true image") offered a simple gesture of kindness to the suffering Jesus. Her compassion serves as a reminder that no act that relieves pain is too small or insignificant.

Father, not my will but yours be done.

7. Jesus Falls a Second Time

We adore you, O Christ, and we praise you, because by your Holy Cross you have redeemed the world.

A second time Jesus is overwhelmed by the journey. Again he manages to get up. How difficult it must have been to summon the strength and courage to go on, knowing full well what lay ahead!

Father, not my will but yours be done.

8. Jesus Meets the Mourning Women

We adore you, O Christ, and we praise you, because by your Holy Cross you have redeemed the world.

Jesus tells the women to weep not for him, but for themselves and their children. He knew they mourned only for "show" and that their sorrow was hollow. Had their hearts been genuine, they would have mourned their own sinfulness.

Father, not my will but yours be done.

9. Jesus Falls a Third Time

We adore you, O Christ, and we praise you, because by your Holy Cross you have redeemed the world.

Falling for the third time under the crushing burden of the cross, Jesus must have been sorely tempted to just lie there. But he drew upon his remaining strength to persevere on his sacrificial journey.

Father, not my will but yours be done.

My God & My All

10. Jesus Is Stripped of His Clothing

We adore you, O Christ, and we praise you, because by your Holy Cross you have redeemed the world.

Jesus felt the sharp agony of old wounds ripped open, adding to the indignity of being publicly stripped of his clothing. Totally vulnerable, totally bereft, he humbled himself on every level for our sake.

Father, not my will but yours be done.

11. Jesus Is Nailed to the Cross

We adore you, O Christ, and we praise you, because by your Holy Cross you have redeemed the world.

Large nails driven through his hands and feet, Jesus suffered even more. The soldiers could have tied him to the cross and he would have died, but they chose this more cruel, more painful way. Still, he forgave them.

Father, not my will but yours be done.

12. Jesus Dies on the Cross

We adore you, O Christ, and we praise you, because by your Holy Cross you have redeemed the world.

The age-old question asked of any suffering echoes through the mystery of the Redemption: why? God, become fully human in Jesus, accepts death in all its suffering. Why does God will this and why is Jesus obedient to the Father's will? The answer is found in the mystery of God's love for each one of us.

Father, not my will but yours be done.

13. Jesus Is Taken from the Cross

We adore you, O Christ, and we praise you, because by your Holy Cross you have redeemed the world.

All life has flowed out, and now all that remains is Jesus' battered and abused body. A soldier pierces his side with a lance, just to make sure he is dead. They can hurt him no more.

Father, not my will but yours be done.

14. Jesus Is Laid in the Tomb

We adore you, O Christ, and we praise you, because by your Holy Cross you have redeemed the world.

For his disciples, Jesus' death and burial meant the end of everything they had hoped for and all of their dreams. What remained were fragments of their faith. Their darkness would soon be transformed, not by their power, but by the glory of God.

Father, not my will but yours be done.

✝

My God & My All

Prayer before the Crucifix

GOOD, KIND and gentle Jesus
I kneel before you.
I see and consider your five wounds.
My eyes behold what David prophesied:
"They have pierced my hands and feet;
they have numbered all my bones."
Engrave upon me this image of yourself.
Fulfill the yearnings of my heart;
give me faith, hope and love, repentance
for all my sins and a true turning
to you for life. ✝

Thanksgiving for the Eucharist

I THANK YOU, Eternal Father, for
giving me as the food of my soul the
Body and Blood of your only-begotten
Son, our Lord Jesus Christ.
May this divine food preserve and in-

My God & My All

crease the union of my soul with you. May it purify me by repressing every evil inclination. Grant that it may be to me a pledge of a glorious resurrection on the last day. O Sacred Heart of Jesus, I love you with all my heart. I am sorry for ever having offended you, and I desire never to offend you again. †

The Rosary

The Rosary begins with the Sign of the Cross and the Apostles' Creed prayed on the crucifix. An Our Father is prayed on each large bead, while a Hail Mary is prayed on each of the small beads. After each group of Hail Marys, the Doxology ("Glory be to the Father, and to the Son...") is prayed.

The Rosary opens, then, with the Sign of the Cross, the Apostles' Creed, an Our Father, three Hail Marys and

My God & My All

the Doxology. The rest of the Rosary is divided into five decades of one Our Father, ten Hail Marys and the Doxology. The Rosary may be concluded with a recitation of the Salve Regina (page 169).

While praying each decade, one meditates on one of the Rosary's fifteen "mysteries," events drawn from the lives of Jesus and Mary. The mysteries of the Rosary are divided into three groups: The Joyful Mysteries, the Sorrowful Mysteries and the Glorious Mysteries.

The Joyful Mysteries

1. The Annunciation—Mary agrees to become the mother of Jesus.

2. The Visitation—Mary travels to the hill country of Judea to visit her cousin Elizabeth.

3. The Birth of Our Lord—Jesus is born to Mary and Joseph in a Bethlehem stable.

4. The Presentation in the Temple—

My God & My All

Jesus is presented in the temple according to Jewish law and Simeon prophesies the Passion.

5. The Finding of Jesus in the Jerusalem temple—Mary and Joseph find Jesus talking to the elders in the temple.

The Sorrowful Mysteries

1. The Agony of Our Lord in the Garden—Jesus prays in great distress over the coming of his Passion and Death.

2. The Scourging of Our Lord—Pilate has Jesus cruelly whipped by the Roman soldiers.

3. The Crowning of Our Lord with a Crown of Thorns—the Roman soldiers press a crown of thorns on Jesus' head while mocking him.

4. Our Lord Carries His Cross—Jesus is made to carry the cross to Calvary.

5. Our Lord Dies on the Cross—after suffering three hours of crucifixion, Jesus dies.

My God & My All

The Glorious Mysteries
1. The Resurrection of Our Lord—Jesus rises from the tomb on Easter morning.
2. The Ascension of Our Lord into Heaven—Jesus returns to the Father forty days after the Resurrection.
3. The Descent of the Holy Spirit—the Advocate promised by Jesus comes to the disciples on Pentecost.
4. The Assumption of Mary into Heaven—united in body and soul, the Mother of Jesus is taken into heaven.
5. The Coronation of Mary—Mary is crowned Queen of Heaven and Earth.

It is traditional to meditate on the Glorious Mysteries when praying the Rosary on Sunday, Wednesday or Saturday; the Joyful Mysteries on Monday and Thursday; and the Sorrowful Mysteries on Tuesday and Friday. †

Salve Regina

HAIL HOLY QUEEN,
Mother of Mercy, our life, our
sweetness and our hope.
To you do we cry, poor banished
children of Eve.
To you do we send up our sighs,
mourning, weeping from this valley of
tears. Turn then, most gracious
Advocate, your eyes of mercy toward us,
and after this our exile show to us the
blessed Fruit of your womb, Jesus.
O clement, O loving, O sweet
Virgin Mary! †

Acknowledgments

Creative Communications for the Parish acknowledges and thanks the following companies for permission to reprint prayers. Every effort has been made to obtain permission for the prayers contained in this book. In the event that copyright information of any prayer is incorrect, corrections will be made in future editions.

Prayer by William Barclay from A PLAIN MAN'S BOOK OF PRAYERS by William Barclay. Used by permission of Christian Classics, Inc.

Prayers by Renee Bartkowski from PRAYERS FOR MARRIED COUPLES by Renee Bartkowski © 1989 by Liguori Publications, Liguori, MO 63057. Reprinted by permission.

Prayers by Michael Buckley, Timothy Dudley-Smith, Basil Naylor and Henri Nouwen from THE NEW BOOK OF CHRISTIAN PRAYERS edited by Tony Castle. Copyright © 1986 by Tony Castle. Reprinted by permission of The Crossroad Publishing Company.

Prayer by Jeanie Gibson reprinted from ANY TIME, LORD by permission of St. Paul Books and Media, Boston, MA 02130.

Prayers by John Gunstone from LORD HEAL ME: A PERSONAL PRAYER COMPANION by John Gunstone © 1988 by John Gunstone. Reprinted by permission of Morehouse Publishing, Wilton, CT. All rights reserved.

Prayer by Edward Hays reprinted with permission from PRAYERS FOR A PLANETARY PILGRIM by Edward Hays (1989: Forest of Peace Books, Inc - Easton, KS 66020).

Prayers by Gabe Huck from A BOOK OF FAMILY PRAYER by Gabe Huck, copyright © 1979 by The Seabury Press, and a prayer by Alan Paton from INSTRUMENT OF THY PEACE by Alan Paton, copyright © 1982 by The Seabury Press, are reprinted by permission of Harper-Collins Publishers.

Prayers by Joe Mannath from THE MYSTERY OF ME by Joe Mannath, copyright © 1990 by Joe Mannath, S.D.B. Used by permission of Doubleday, a division of Bantam Doubleday Dell Publishing Group, Inc.

Prayer by Thomas Merton from THOUGHTS IN SOLITUDE by Thomas Merton. Copyright © 1958 by The Abbey of Our Lady of Gethsemani. Renewal copyright © 1986 by Trustees of the Thomas Merton Legacy Trust. Reprinted by permission of Farrar, Straus and Giroux, Inc.

Prayers by Huub Oosterhuis from YOUR WORD IS NEAR by Huub Oosterhuis, copyright © Huub Oosterhuis. Published by Paulist Press. Used by permission.

Prayers by Arnaldo Pangrazzi from YOUR WORDS IN PRAYER IN TIME OF ILLNESS, by Fr. A. Pangrazzi, O.S. Cam., Alba House, New York, 1982. Used by permission.

Prayers by Pope John Paul II from PRAYERS OF POPE JOHN PAUL II edited by John F. McDonald. Copyright St. Paul Publications © 1982. Reprinted by permission of The Crossroad Publishing Company.

Prayer by John Powers is reprinted with permission from IF THEY COULD SPEAK: TEN WITNESSES TO THE PASSION OF JESUS, copyright © 1990 by John D. Powers, C.P., (paper, $4.95), published by Twenty-Third Publications, P.O. Box 180, Mystic, CT 06355. Toll free: 1-800-321-0411.

Prayer by Karl Rahner, S.J. from PRAYERS FOR A LIFETIME edited by Albert Raffelt, copyright © 1984 by The Crossroad Publishing Company. Reprinted by permission of The Crossroad Publishing Company.

Index of Authors

Barclay, William, 65
Bartkowski, Renee, 66, 108, 119
Buckley, Michael, 110
Bernardin, Cardinal Joseph, 90

Dudley-Smith, Timothy, 82

Finley, Mitch, 116
de Foucauld, Charles, 45

Gibson, Jeanie, 136
Gunstone, John, 64, 68, 70

Hays, Edward, 143
Huck, Gabe, 127, 128

Mannath, Joe, 11, 52, 111, 123
Merton, Thomas, 46

Naylor, Basil, 33
Neilsen, Mark, 8, 10, 24, 37, 40, 59, 80, 88, 91, 99, 135, 141, 146, 147, 149, 151
Nouwen, Henri, 57

Oosterhuis, Huub, 86, 96

Pangrazzi, Arnaldo, 71, 73, 74
Paton, Alan, 87

Pope John Paul II, 114, 139
Powers, John, 75

Rahner, Karl, 144
Royer, Jean, 3, 14, 38

St. Augustine, 16
St. Catherine of Siena, 27
St. Francis of Assisi, 23, 63
St. Ignatius Loyola, 127
St. Peter Canisius, 82
Summers, Nancy, 36, 51

Vanek, Elizabeth-Anne, *psalms*: 2, 26, 32, 35, 44, 48, 50, 55, 62, 78, 94, 101, 106, 122, 134; *prayers*: 5, 6, 28, 31, 47, 69, 79, 85, 89, 98, 115, 140, 145

Zralek, Marguerite, 64

A Treasury of
LIVING FAITH
Catholic Devotions For Every Day of the Year

This **totally new** Treasury is a top-quality, hardcover book with the best devotions from past issues of **LIVING FAITH** (and **Living Words**). An earlier book of daily devotions was popular with many readers. Now we're offering this new **Treasury**, which we're sure you'll cherish for yourself or will enjoy giving as a very special gift.

✔ • 384 pages • $12.95 + $2 shipping • **Code TL-F**

Book Orders • Creative Communications for the Parish
10300 Watson Road
St. Louis, MO 63127

The most widely circulated Catholic devotional booklet!

LIVING FAITH
Daily Catholic Devotions

- Inexpensive
- New each quarter
- Pocket-size or large, easy-to-read editions

Each quarterly issue of *Living Faith* provides daily devotions based on the Mass readings, with selections from contemporary Catholic authors such as Henri J.M. Nouwen, John Powell and Thomas Keating as well as spiritual leaders like Pope John Paul II and Mother Teresa. Other devotions are contributed by Christians from all walks of life: lay, clergy and religious.

For information on ordering, write:
Subscription Department
Creative Communications for the Parish
10300 Watson Road
St. Louis, MO 63127